The Inside GUIDE

FAMOUS NATIVE AMERICANS

Geronimo

By Laura L. Sullivan

Cavendish
Square

New York

Published in 2021 by Cavendish Square Publishing, LLC
243 5th Avenue, Suite 136, New York, NY 10016

Copyright © 2021 by Cavendish Square Publishing, LLC

First Edition

Library of Congress Cataloging-in-Publication Data

Names: Sullivan, Laura L., author.
Title: Geronimo / Laura L. Sullivan.
Description: First edition. | New York, NY : Cavendish Square Publishing, LLC, 2021. | Series: The inside guide: Famous Native Americans | Includes bibliographical references and index.
Identifiers: LCCN 2019042246 (print) | LCCN 2019042247 (ebook) | ISBN 9781502650580 (library binding) | ISBN 9781502650566 (paperback) | ISBN 9781502650573 (set) | ISBN 9781502650597 (ebook)
Subjects: LCSH: Geronimo, 1829-1909–Juvenile literature. | Apache Indians–Kings and rulers–Biography–Juvenile literature. | Apache Indians–Wars–Juvenile literature.
Classification: LCC E99.A6 S87 2021 (print) | LCC E99.A6 (ebook) | DDC 979.004/97250092 [B]–dc23
LC record available at https://lccn.loc.gov/2019042246
LC ebook record available at https://lccn.loc.gov/2019042247

Editor: Kristen Susienka
Copy Editor: Rebecca Rohan
Designer: Deanna Paternostro

The photographs in this book are used by permission and through the courtesy of: Cover, pp. 7, 8, 10, 29 (left) Everett Historical/Shutterstock.com; pp. 4, 13 © CORBIS/Corbis via Getty Images; p. 6 © The Holbarn Archive/Bridgeman Images; p. 11 Michael Barera/Wikimedia Commons; pp. 12-13 Universal History Archive/UIG via Getty Images; p. 14 Glasshouse Vintage/Universal History Archive/Universal Images Group via Getty Images; p. 15 ~riley/Wikimedia Commons; p. 16 Private Collection/© Look and Learn/Bridgeman Images; pp. 18, 29 (right) Universal History Archive/Universal Images Group via Getty Images. p. 19 Pictorial Press Ltd/Alamy Stock Photo; p. 20 C.S. Fly/Library of Congress/Corbis/VCG via Getty Images; p. 21 The Print Collector/Print Collector/Getty Images; p. 22 Transcendental Graphics/Getty Images; p. 23 MPI/Getty Images; p. 24 Time Life Pictures/US Signal Corps/The LIFE Picture Collection/Getty Images; p. 25 Bettmann/Bettmann/Getty Images; p. 26 Museum of Science and Industry, Chicago/Getty Images; p. 28 (top left) DEA/ICAS94/De Agostini/Getty Images; p. 28 (top right) Edward S. Curtis/PhotoQuest/Getty Images; p. 28 (bottom left) Education Images/UIG/Universal Images Group/Getty Images Plus/Getty Images; p. 28 (bottom right) Courtesy of the Library of Congress.

Some of the images in this book illustrate individuals who are models. The depictions do not imply actual situations or events.

CPSIA compliance information: Batch #CS20CSQ: For further information contact Cavendish Square Publishing LLC, New York, New York, at 1-877-980-4450.

Printed in the United States of America

Find us on

CONTENTS

Geronimo was an Apache leader and fighter.

A LEGENDARY FIGURE

*T*hroughout history, many people have led important lives or done great things for causes in which they believe. Some people have spoken up for the rights of people in their community. Others have tried to gain more respect for their ways of life and beliefs.

Great Native Americans

Perhaps one of the most overlooked groups of people in the history of the United States is Native Americans. There have been many native people who have led amazing lives. They've helped their communities, and they've shaped the world into a better place. You've probably heard of some famous Native Americans, like Pocahontas and Squanto. Others, like Sequoyah and Geronimo, might not be as familiar. Geronimo was a Native American who fought to protect the people and way of life that mattered most to him. In doing this, he became an important part of American history.

Geronimo

Geronimo's story is important to understanding how fighting between groups changed America during the 1800s and 1900s. Geronimo was

This illustration shows Mexican soldiers fighting Spanish soldiers to gain Mexico's independence.

6

born in what was then Mexico. Mexico once belonged to Spain, but in 1821, it became its own country. War was much of what Geronimo knew during his life. He and his tribe fought many battles against other groups.

In 1848, parts of Mexico became parts of the United States. The United States wanted more land, including the land Geronimo and his people lived on. US leaders passed laws that forced Native Americans to move across the country, far away from their homes. Geronimo didn't want to move. He spent many years fighting with the US government to stay on his people's land.

People who knew Geronimo had different opinions about him. Some people thought he

Theodore Roosevelt was president when Geronimo was alive. Here he is in 1903, while on a tour of the western United States.

THE MEXICAN-AMERICAN WAR AND ITS AFTERMATH

One of the most significant conflicts during Geronimo's early life was the Mexican-American War. It was fought from 1846 to 1848. Members of the Mexican army fought the US Army for land. In the end, the United States gained land that today makes up parts of the western and southwestern United States. Places like Arizona, New Mexico, and California were given to the United States in the **Treaty** of Guadalupe Hidalgo, which ended the war.

The war affected many native communities living in that part of the world. Some native groups helped the US Army. For example, Mangas Coloradas, an Apache chief, signed a treaty with the US Army that let the army travel through his people's territory in peace.

However, after its victory, the US government treated the native people and their lands badly. Many native societies would never be the same. Geronimo himself was changed by this war and all that came after.

This scene shows the Battle of Palo Alto, which happened during the Mexican-American War.

was a hero. Others thought he was a pest. Still, he fought bravely and tried to do the right thing for his community. Later in his life, he became a celebrity. People remembered Geronimo's name and came from around the United States to see him.

Geronimo remains a legendary figure in history today. His story is one filled with sadness but also hope and determination. He has inspired generations of native and non-native people, and his story is one that will not be forgotten.

Geronimo was a member of the Apache tribe. He posed for this photograph in 1898.

A HERO OF
THE APACHE

Geronimo was born in June 1829 in a canyon in what was then Mexico. His small **band** of people was called the Bendonkohe. They were part of the Apache tribe. His band was the smallest of the tribe, but it had fierce warriors to protect its people.

Early Life

Geronimo grew up during a time of change in the world, especially North America. Mexico was fighting many battles against native people living in the country. Geronimo's people fought with the Mexican government. They also fought with other native groups living near them. The Comanche and Navajo were their enemies.

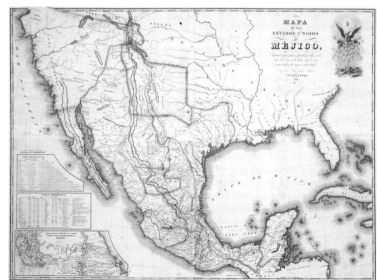

This map of Mexico was made in 1828.

11

Mexican Attack

Mexico wanted the native people's land for itself. The Apache didn't think the land should belong to Mexico. For years, the Apache struggled to protect their land.

When Geronimo was 17, he married a woman named Alope. They had three children. They were happy, but one day, he and other men in his tribe went to another town to trade. While they were gone, Mexican soldiers attacked his home. Geronimo's mother, his wife, and his children were killed. Geronimo was **devastated**. His whole family was taken from him.

After that, he wanted **revenge**. He spent his life fighting for his people.

Fighting the United States

In 1848, Mexico lost a war with the United States and had to give up some land. The Americans now owned Apache land where Geronimo lived. Gold was discovered there, which brought settlers to the area. They started farming and mining there.

By now, Geronimo was a respected adult and an accomplished warrior. He led **raids** against other native groups and American settlers who built homes nearby.

To control the Native Americans, the United States started creating reservations. Reservations are areas that the US government sets aside for Native American tribes to live on. Some tribes agreed to treaties to stop fighting. They also said they would move to reservations. They thought they would be safe and

Fast Fact

The Apache were great horse riders. Native groups first learned of horses from the Spanish, who ruled what is now Mexico from the 1500s to the 1800s.

The Apache lived in homemade houses. This family sits in front of their house on an Arizona reservation in 1886.

protected there. Geronimo went to live on a reservation in San Carlos, Arizona.

Life on the reservation was hard. The Apache weren't used to living in one place. Apache tribes traveled the land. Staying in one place went against their traditions. Also, sometimes the tribes weren't given what they were promised. Some Apache starved. Others died of diseases.

Escape from the Reservation

Geronimo escaped from the reservation three times in the 1870s and 1880s. He and his followers fled to the Mexican-US border. They hid in the mountains known as the Sierra Madre. From there, they raided both Mexican and US towns and ranches.

US soldiers chased them and fought them for many years. Finally, Geronimo was caught. He agreed to **surrender** in 1886.

Geronimo and the others were sent far from their homelands. Geronimo was sent to Florida. He was a prisoner in Pensacola. However, he also became a tourist attraction. People wanted to see the fierce and famous warrior.

Geronimo (*front row, third from right*) and other Apache prisoners were sent by train to Florida. His son sits to his left in a matching shirt.

Wild West shows featured Native Americans, cowboys, and horses.

Life as a Prisoner

Later, Geronimo was moved to Alabama, and then to Oklahoma. The families of the Apache prisoners had been kept in other places. Many died of diseases. Geronimo was reunited with his family. Over time, he was allowed a little more freedom. He took part in the 1904 World's Fair in Saint Louis, Missouri, and a Wild West show. However, he was always guarded by soldiers when he traveled.

In 1909, Geronimo was thrown from his horse. He lay in the freezing cold overnight. He soon died of pneumonia. On his deathbed, he said he wished he'd never surrendered. He said, "I should have fought until I was the last man alive."

THE APACHE

The Apache are a group of several Native American tribes. They are from the southwestern part of what's now the United States.

In the past, the Apache were **nomadic**. This means they didn't build lasting cities. Instead, they set up villages for a while, then moved on. At one time, the Apache hunted bison in the Great Plains. Later, they mostly moved to more mountainous areas.

After many years of fighting with the Spanish, Mexicans, and Americans, most Apache were forced to live on reservations. Many Apache still live on reservations in New Mexico or Arizona. However, they can live wherever they want today.

Fast Fact
Nearly 25 percent of the US Army participated in the search and capture of Geronimo between 1885 and 1886.

This is Geronimo's grave at Fort Sill in Oklahoma.

This painting shows an Apache tribe riding through the Southwest.

A CHANGING WORLD

In the 1800s, many Americans wanted the United States to stretch from one coast to the other. This idea was called **Manifest Destiny**. People who believed in Manifest Destiny often didn't care about Native Americans who lived in parts of the United States that hadn't yet been settled by white people. As more settlers arrived, they fought with Native American groups and pushed them from their homes. Geronimo fought back against this.

New Opportunities, New Problems

Also in the 1800s, new technologies were appearing in the United States. Trains became important for sending people and supplies across the country. The country was connected like never before, but not everyone was affected positively by these changes.

Fast Fact

A magazine called the *Democratic Review* first used the term "Manifest Destiny" in an article published in 1845.

As years went on, Native American groups were pushed further aside. In 1830, the United States passed the Indian Removal Act. This meant all Native Americans east of the Mississippi could be forced to move their communities far from white settlers.

The transcontinental railroad brought the East Coast and West Coast together but displaced many Native American communities living on the route.

Many people in native communities were angry about this. They didn't want to leave their homes just because white settlers wanted to live there too. They fought back, but it did little to persuade the US government.

More acts were passed. The Homestead Act of 1862 had a major impact on Native American communities and settlers in the West,

Fast Fact

Grover Cleveland was president of the United States from 1885 to 1889 and again from 1893 to 1897. It's said that when Geronimo surrendered, Cleveland said he'd prefer Geronimo to be executed. In the end, Geronimo was kept a prisoner of war until his death.

including Geronimo. The act encouraged white settlers to move to areas like the Great Plains that had once been home to mostly Native Americans.

All of these actions by the government affected native people like Geronimo. Throughout the 1800s and 1900s, most tribes were forced to go to reservations. Living on a reservation meant they had to change their way of life. They had to leave their homes. They were supposed to be protected

This is a well-known photograph of Geronimo.

and given supplies, but in reality, many suffered greatly. They got sick, or they didn't have enough food to eat.

The United States sometimes broke promises it made to the Native Americans. The government took back land it said it would give to the tribes. This land was used to build cities, homes, or railroads.

In the late 1800s, Geronimo and other Native Americans had a difficult choice. Should they fight for their way of life, or should they accept peace even if they couldn't live in their homes or celebrate their traditions? Geronimo chose to fight.

War or Peace?

One thing that made having peace difficult was that the Apache people were many separate tribes. Sometimes, one tribe would want to stop fighting, but then other tribes would keep fighting. The US government often saw all Apache as members of the same group. When one group attacked, the army would attack or punish any Apache they could find. It didn't matter if they were innocent or not.

Geronimo was a member of the Chiricahua tribe within the Apache group. After 10 years of fighting, one of the leaders, Cochise, agreed to move the tribe to a reservation. Later, Geronimo and many followers left the reservation. They were angry with how the reservation was run. They often didn't have enough to eat. They wanted to live off the land they had always known.

Geronimo's story ended the same way as many other Native Americans at the time who tried to fight to keep their way of life. In 1886, Geronimo and 24 warriors were hiding near the Mexican border. The US Army had tried for months to catch them. Finally, they sent many soldiers, Native American scouts, and volunteers after them. Geronimo was caught and later surrendered.

Geronimo (*center*) waits with other Apache warriors in 1886.

THE GREAT STRUGGLE WITH CROOK

Major General George F. Crook was born in 1828 in Ohio. He graduated from the military training school West Point in 1852. After that, his main job was building forts and protecting settlers in the Northwest.

The **American Civil War** began in 1861, and Crook fought for the Union. He fought in several battles. Afterward, he was ordered first to California and then to Arizona. His mission in Arizona was to move all Apache to reservations. He left Arizona for a few years but was called back in 1882 with a mission specifically focused on Geronimo.

Crook had to stop Geronimo from attacking settlers and soldiers and resisting life on the reservation. However, Geronimo proved a difficult opponent. Until 1886, Crook and his men sought out him and other Apache in the mountains and deserts. Geronimo escaped him, but Crook and his group did capture 500 other Apache and moved them to the San Carlos Reservation. In 1886, Crook was replaced by General Nelson A. Miles, who did capture Geronimo.

Near the end of his life, Crook had a change of heart. He came to understand the Native American struggle and tried to stand up against wrongs done to them, especially the Apache. Crook died in 1890 in Chicago, Illinois.

Shown here is George Crook.

Geronimo was often photographed holding a gun.

GERONIMO'S LEGACY

Geronimo is usually remembered as a hero of the Apache people. Most of the Apache understood why he fought. First, he fought for revenge after his family was killed. His heart was broken, and his life had changed forever. His family was innocent. They didn't deserve to die. Later, Americans threatened Geronimo's people, so he helped his people fight against them. Geronimo attacked others because he wanted to protect the people he loved.

Geronimo was dedicated to his family.

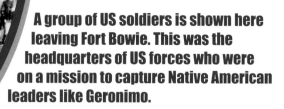

A group of US soldiers is shown here leaving Fort Bowie. This was the headquarters of US forces who were on a mission to capture Native American leaders like Geronimo.

Violence Everywhere

Many recognize Geronimo's heroism. However, the things he did could be very violent and cruel. He killed soldiers, but he also targeted farmers, ranchers, and settlers. His warriors sometimes killed women and children—people who weren't fighting.

Of course, the Mexican army and the US government were doing similar things. Both sides killed young people and families. It was a horrible time. Neither side wanted to show mercy.

Not All Good

Many think that Geronimo's actions were justified. He was hurting because of the bad things happening to his people. However, others think that violence isn't a good way to deal with anger and that there are better ways to gain peace. Some people in Geronimo's tribe wanted to talk to members of the US government to solve their problems. These talks sometimes led to treaties. Over time, though, promises in the treaties were broken. Many native people lost their faith in the US government.

Fast Fact

Legend says that Geronimo got his name after he attacked a Mexican soldier. The soldier called for help from Saint Jerome (*Jeronimo* in Spanish). It was a name his enemies gave him, and it brought fear to many people.

24

Geronimo (*center*) was a prisoner of war at a reservation in Oklahoma.

Some members of Geronimo's tribe believed his constant attacking and retreating made the fighting longer and more painful. When Geronimo and his followers escaped from the reservations, it made life harder for those who remained. When some Apache fought, the United States treated all Apache worse. Those searching for and fighting

GERONIMO!

Geronimo's name has become part of **parachuting** tradition. Often, when someone jumps out of a plane, they shout "Geronimo!" as they leap.

There are different stories about how this started. In one legend, US Army paratroopers (soldiers who use parachutes) were nervous before a jump. Parachutes were a new invention. If the parachute failed, the soldiers could die. To calm their nerves, they watched a Western (a movie about the American West) the night before a big jump. Geronimo was a character in the movie. The next day, he was fresh in their minds. They shouted Geronimo's name to show their bravery.

Another story tells that, to escape, Geronimo once made his horse leap off a steep cliff. He yelled his own name as he jumped. The soldiers chasing him weren't brave enough to follow, so Geronimo escaped.

Parachuters jumping from planes often yell "Geronimo!"

Geronimo sometimes got help from other members of Apache groups. They were scouts or interpreters.

Geronimo Today

Today, Geronimo is remembered for several things. Above all, he's known as a strong warrior. He fought with bravery for most of his life. He stood up for his people. He tried to do what was right for them.

Sometimes, Geronimo is also remembered as a holy man with magical powers. One story says he led his people into a cave when soldiers were chasing them. The soldiers never saw them come out, but later, the soldiers saw them far away. Some believe Geronimo used magic to escape from the trap. Whether the story is true or not, we will never know.

Many things are named after Geronimo. Three towns in the United States have his name. His

Fast Fact

Geronimo didn't write his autobiography. Instead, he dictated it to an interpreter, and then the interpreter told another person, who wrote the story down in English.

picture appeared on a US stamp. At least four movies tell his story. His own words also paint a picture of his life. A few years before he died, Geronimo's autobiography was published. It's called *Geronimo: His Own Story*. Geronimo remains a legend today.

THINK ABOUT IT!

Use these questions to help you think more deeply about this topic.

1. Why was violence such a major part of the relationship between Native Americans and white settlers?

2. How did new technologies affect Native Americans living during Geronimo's lifetime?

3. How could Geronimo have acted differently to bring about peace for his people?

4. How do you think Geronimo's actions would be interpreted if they happened today?

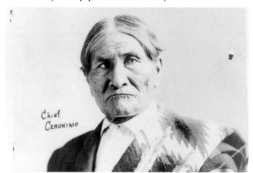

TIMELINE

Geronimo's Life	World Events

June 1829
Geronimo is born near the border of Arizona and New Mexico.

May 28, 1830
The Indian Removal Act is passed.

1846
Geronimo marries his first wife.

1846–1848
The Mexican-American War is fought.

1849–1886
The Apache Wars are fought.

March 5, 1858
Mexican soldiers kill Geronimo's wife, children, and mother.

1879
The Apache begin to rebel against the reservation system.

September 4, 1886
Geronimo officially surrenders to US soldiers.

February 17, 1909
Geronimo dies at Fort Sill, Oklahoma.

1939
US Army paratroopers begin shouting "Geronimo!" when they parachute.

29

GLOSSARY

American Civil War: A war fought from 1861 to 1865 between the North and the South in the United States over slavery and other issues.

band: A group of people connected to a larger group but operating independently.

devastated: Extremely sad and heartbroken.

dictate: To tell a story or speak words that are meant to be written down.

Manifest Destiny: A way of thinking in the 1800s that all land from the Atlantic Ocean to the Pacific Ocean should belong to the United States.

nomadic: Moving from place to place, not living in a settled city.

parachute: To jump from a plane using a special fabric balloon to slow the fall.

raid: A sudden, quick attack on a village or city.

rebel: A person who is against a leader or government.

revenge: The act of harming someone because they caused you harm first.

stereotypical: Relating to a way of thinking that incorrectly views all members of a group as the same. Stereotypes are often, but not always, negative.

surrender: To give up or stop fighting.

treaty: A formal agreement between two countries or groups.

FIND OUT MORE

Books

Lowery, Linda. *Native Peoples of the Southwest*. Minneapolis, MN: Lerner Classroom, 2017.

Stearns, Peter N., and Philip Baselice, consultants. *American History: A Visual Encyclopedia*. New York, NY: DK Publishing, 2019.

Weil, Ann. *Geronimo*. Portsmouth, NH: Heinemann, 2012.

Websites

Encyclopedia Britannica: Geronimo
www.britannica.com/biography/Geronimo
This website gives a detailed history of Geronimo, his life, and his mission.

Geronimo History and Early Photographs
www.youtube.com/watch?v=JukBVfMe3GM
See authentic photos of Geronimo and other Apache as you learn about his history.

Native Americans: Apache Peoples
www.ducksters.com/history/native_american_apache.php
This Ducksters site introduces kids to Apache culture and includes a quiz and links to more information.

Publisher's note to educators and parents: Our editors have carefully reviewed these websites to ensure that they are suitable for students. Many websites change frequently, however, and we cannot guarantee that a site's future contents will continue to meet our high standards of quality and educational value. Be advised that students should be closely supervised whenever they access the Internet.

INDEX